CAROL M. HIGHSMITH AND TED LANDPHAIR

CHICAGO

A PHOTOGRAPHIC TOUR

CRESCENT BOOKS
NEW YORK

Daniel Chester
French's reproduction
of his Republic statue
(page 1) stands in
Jackson Park. It
marked the twenty-
fifth anniversary of the
World's Columbian
Exposition. The
original, temporary
statue, which towered
over the fair's reflecting
basin, looked much like
the Statue of Liberty
and sent a similar
message of welcome.
PAGES 2–3: Bucking-
ham Fountain, in its
own plaza along the
lakefront east of Grant
Park, was the world's
largest decorative
fountain when it was
given to the city by
philanthropist Kate
Sturges Buckingham in
1927. To the delight of
Chicagoans and
visitors with cameras
alike, it is spectacularly
activated from May 1
to October 1 and is
illuminated at night.

THE AUTHORS GRATEFULLY ACKNOWLEDGE
THE SERVICES, ACCOMMODATIONS, AND SUPPORT PROVIDED BY
HILTON HOTELS CORPORATION
AND
THE PALMER HOUSE HILTON
IN CONNECTION WITH THE COMPLETION OF THIS BOOK.

————

This 1997 edition is published by Crescent Books,
a division of Random House Value Publishing, Inc.,
201 East 50th Street, New York, N.Y. 10022.

Crescent Books and colophon are trademarks of
Random House Value Publishing, Inc.

Random House
New York • Toronto • London • Sydney • Auckland
http://www.randomhouse.com/

Printed and bound in China

Library of Congress Cataloging-in-Publication Data
Highsmith, Carol M., 1946–
Chicago / Carol M. Highsmith and Ted Landphair.
p.   cm. — (A photographic tour)
ISBN 0–517–18331–5 (hc: alk. paper)
1. Chicago (Ill.)—Tours. 2. Chicago (Ill.)—Pictorial works.
I. Landphair, Ted, 1942– . II. Title. III. Series.
F548.18.H54   1997
917.73´110443—dc20   96–43089
CIP

8   7   6   5   4   3   2

————

Designed by Robert L. Wiser, Archetype Press, Inc., Washington, D.C.

All photographs by Carol M. Highsmith unless otherwise credited:
map by XNR Productions, page 5; painting by Robert Mark Melnick, page 6;
Harold Washington Library Center, pages 8–21

The authors acknowledge the superb assistance of the Chicago Office of
Tourism, the historical guidance of Don Klimovich, and the hospitality of
Berghoff's Restaurant, Gino's East, and Cafe Ba-Ba-Reeba. They also extend
their deep gratitude to Chicagophile Sara Akerlund, whose knowledge of the
city's hidden treasures made many of these photographs possible.

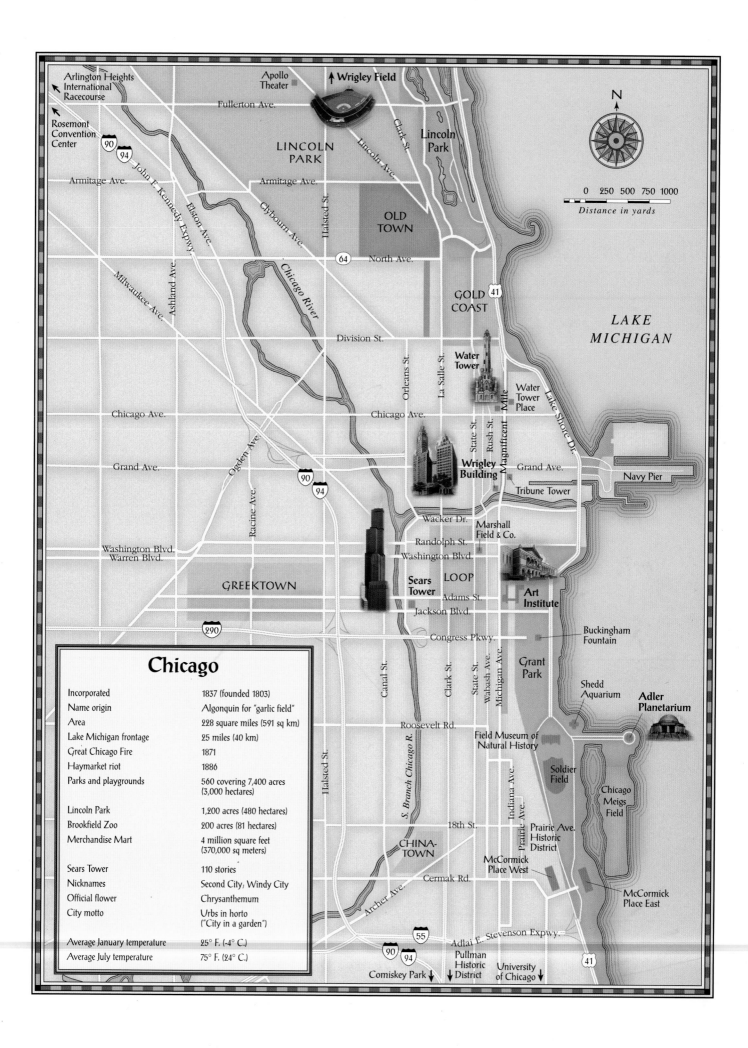

Chicago

Incorporated	1837 (founded 1803)
Name origin	Algonquin for "garlic field"
Area	228 square miles (591 sq km)
Lake Michigan frontage	25 miles (40 km)
Great Chicago Fire	1871
Haymarket riot	1886
Parks and playgrounds	560 covering 7,400 acres (3,000 hectares)
Lincoln Park	1,200 acres (480 hectares)
Brookfield Zoo	200 acres (81 hectares)
Merchandise Mart	4 million square feet (370,000 sq meters)
Sears Tower	110 stories
Nicknames	Second City; Windy City
Official flower	Chrysanthemum
City motto	Urbs in horto ("City in a garden")
Average January temperature	25° F. (-4° C.)
Average July temperature	75° F. (24° C.)

Arlington Heights International Racecourse

Rosemont Convention Center

Apollo Theater

↑ Wrigley Field

Lincoln Park

N

0   250 500 750 1000
Distance in yards

Fullerton Ave.

LINCOLN PARK

Lincoln Ave.

Clark St.

Armitage Ave.

Armitage Ave.

OLD TOWN

John F. Kennedy Expwy.

Elston Ave.

Clybourn Ave.

Halsted St.

64

North Ave.

GOLD COAST

41

LAKE MICHIGAN

Milwaukee Ave.

Ashland Ave.

Chicago River

Division St.

Water Tower

Orleans St.

La Salle St.

Water Tower Place

Chicago Ave.

Chicago Ave.

State St.

Rush St.

Magnificent Mile

Lake Shore Dr.

Grand Ave.

Ogden Ave.

90 94

Grand Ave.

Wrigley Building

Tribune Tower

Navy Pier

Racine Ave.

Wacker Dr.

Marshall Field & Co.

Washington Blvd.
Warren Blvd.

Randolph St.

Washington Blvd.

Sears Tower

LOOP

Art Institute

GREEKTOWN

Adams St.

Jackson Blvd.

290

Congress Pkwy.

Buckingham Fountain

Grant Park

Shedd Aquarium

Adler Planetarium

Canal St.

Clark St.

State St.

Wabash Ave.

Michigan Ave.

Roosevelt Rd.

Field Museum of Natural History

Soldier Field

Chicago Meigs Field

Halsted St.

S. Branch Chicago R.

18th St.

Indiana Ave.

Prairie Ave.

Prairie Ave. Historic District

CHINA-TOWN

McCormick Place West

McCormick Place East

Archer Ave.

Cermak Rd.

55

Adlai E. Stevenson Expwy.

90 94

Pullman Historic District

Comiskey Park ↓

University of Chicago ↓

41

CHICAGO. THE CITY OF THE BIG SHOULDERS, still "stormy, husky, brawling" as Carl Sandberg extolled it, still rolling up its sleeves and getting to work, though assuredly no longer "hog butcher for the world." Where ninety city blocks of pens and slaughterhouses once stood on the South Side, only Daniel Burnham's massive stone entrance portal remains in a nondescript industrial park. A century has gone by since ten thousand visitors a day came to watch brawny men with sledgehammers deliver the *coup de grace* to bellowing hogs and steers at the Armour and Swift operations of the Union Stock Yards. Chicago has put on considerable finery and a few airs. But this boisterous, boastful, teeming, remarkably scrubbed prairie city is still the big dog of the Heartland.

Chicago is a place of lush green parks (five-hundred-fifty-two citywide—many right downtown), of slate lake waters, of quirky black-and-white bands on the caps of cops. Of yellow taxis that keep a move on, orange reflections of sunsets off shimmering skyscrapers, sienna festival costumes, tan walls surprisingly free from the scrawls of "urban artists." Of red Bulls heads and Bears crooked "Cs" everywhere, elegant brownstone villas, blue beer signs in tavern windows. Of white snowflakes as early as September and as late as May, swirling across the river and up Michigan Avenue and soon mashed to gray; of neon rainbows along the Magnificent Mile and in the passenger tunnel of O'Hare International Airport; and thriving, polyglot neighborhoods.

Chicagoans love their superlatives—the nation's first skyscraper (the Home Insurance Company Building, 1885) and the first comprehensive municipal plan (Burnham again, 1909). Most Nobel laureates; world's largest private building (the Merchandise Mart with ninety acres of floor space); best hot dog and pizza. Largest indoor aquarium, one of the world's last free zoos, most massive outdoor food festival. Civilization's largest free library. Even the largest Tiffany dome anywhere, atop the old central library, which has been transformed into another first— a free municipal cultural and performing-arts center. Chicago even has the only river in the world that was trained to run backward; in 1900, using a system of locks, engineers turned the flow of the Chicago River, preferring to transport the city's sewage to St. Louis rather than into Lake Michigan. Tallest building? You bet: Sears Tower, agrees everyone in "Chicagoland."

Chicago's wind does not just whip or whistle or mournfully howl. It fairly screams off the plains and through the city's high-rise canyons. Stolid Chicagoans simply hitch up their scarves and bend to their tasks with the same good nature that they weather a summer hailstorm or another Cubs collapse. Sure, it's cold, but Chicago is so "livable." Who can doubt it, with thirty-four museums, well over six thousand restaurants, more than two hundred annual parades, twenty-nine miles of lakefront, including fifteen miles of bathing beaches, and eighteen miles of bicycle paths? Or unexpected delights, like a summer public-art program that plops down whimsical statuary—horses, rabbits, elephants, surreal human figures, and all manner of other bizarre bronze forms—into Grant Park and the city's airports and train station, sometimes by helicopter. How satisfying is it, too, to come upon what the *Tribune* calls "a patch of peace" in the courtyard of DuSable High School in the projects neighborhood of South Chicago. Designed by students and overseen by an architect, the "Urban Ecology Sanctuary" includes water pools; roaming chickens, pheasants, peacocks, and a goat; and a quiet corner to mourn the neighborhood's murdered children.

Of course Chicagoans are used to living in an outdoor sculpture and architecture arcade. Do they even notice, any longer, Alexander Calder's fifty-three-foot steel "flamingo" in the

Chicago graphic artist Robert Mark Melnick executed this twelve-foot-by-seven-foot oil painting of the Court of Honor from the 1893 World's Columbian Exposition. It is displayed in the main dining room of Berghoff's Restaurant on West Adams Street downtown. The "Great White City" set in motion a "City Beautiful" movement across the nation.

This early stereopticon view from Rush Street shows a prosperous Chicago River wharf. During the terrible 1871 fire, some ships weighed anchor and were spared; others stayed put and burned like matchsticks.

plaza of three downtown federal buildings, Claes Oldenburg's one-hundred-foot-tall column in the shape of a baseball bat outside the offices of the Social Security Administration, and Pablo Picasso's untitled steel creature in the Daley Center Plaza? Not to mention works with names like *Splash* and *Monument with Standing Beast*. But it's not all modern art. Since 1927, the city has unofficially marked the beginning and end of summer with the rejuvenation of the Clarence Buckingham Fountain in Grant Park. Modeled after a fountain in Versailles, it has three basins carved of pink marble. Flanked by four massive pairs of bronze sea horses, the fountain recirculates half a million gallons of water through 133 jets.

Cynics have gloated over those years when Chicago led the nation in judges and councilmen on the take, votes by dead people, numbers of speakeasies, deaths by tommy gun, and excessive-force complaints against its police. The "rackets"—shakedowns of citizens and small businesses for a percentage of their earnings, a portion of which were used to pay off the very authorities the victims might go to for redress—were once a Chicago institution. But the end of Prohibition, crackdowns by local and federal gangbusters, and the imprisonment or violent death of prominent mobsters broke the Syndicates, though the roots of corruption would periodically sprout new tendrils. Like people in every urban center, Chicagoans worry about random criminal acts, but they're more often vocal about potholes and expressway construction detours, the inadequacies of a local team's coach, and the cost of a toll call. Chicago's phone company was one of the first in the nation to charge thirty cents for a pay-booth call.

There's not much else to pout about. Unfold a map of Chicago and you're struck by the profusion of parks in every quadrant of the city—Peterson, Horner, Warren, Chase, Jensen, Humboldt, Garfield, Sherman, Hamilton, and on and on. Many are connected by a belt line of boulevards that runs west from Lincoln Park, turns south all the way to Gage Park, then back east to Jackson Park at the lake. It's little wonder that Chicago's motto is *Urbs in Horto:* "City in a Garden." Inside it are myriad neighborhoods—not suburbs, but officially named communities that resemble a patchwork of small towns locked within the city: Hyde Park, Lincoln Square, Rogers Park, Old Town, and seventy-four others.

Chicagoans of all faiths are likely to talk about their local parishes. Take Saint Benedict's Church in the city's North Center, for example. Saint Ben's developed as a "territorial parish," drawing worshipers from several ethnic groups. This is not so for many others. Saint Michael's in Old Town, for one, served the city's first large German community in the 1870s; hence its glorious German baroque interior. In classic neighborhood succession, as the Germans grew more prosperous they drifted northwest out the diagonal Lincoln Avenue, and the Irish and Poles moved in. Go out Lincoln Avenue three or so miles, and you come to Saint Alphonsus, a Gothic church with a more elegant exterior that served the second pocket of German settlement. Still later, out Lincoln at Lawrence, in what was then farmland, Saint Mathias was built to further serve the German progression.

Now you still find German beerhouses near Saint Alphonsus and Saint Mathias, but you also encounter Korean grocery stores and Mexican gift shops. Poles, too, moved northwest out a diagonal, Milwaukee Avenue. The Polish Center and two big Polish churches remain near

Milwaukee and Chicago avenues, but the crux of the community has moved farther out into Avondale, where a customer at a Polish bakery will hear English only if he speaks it first. It's still true that this area, and Jefferson Park farther out Milwaukee Avenue, shelter the highest concentration of Poles outside Warsaw.

With these migrations, Chicago's tightly bunched European character became diluted, and the city, in the view of many, was invigorated. It has had a thriving Mexican population—even a Mexican chamber of commerce—for a century, and the shopkeepers of Little Village on the South Side have used ornamental gateways and imaginative street furniture to welcome outsiders. Lawrence Avenue—"Little Seoul"—is filled with Korean shops. Thousands of people from the Indian subcontinent coalesced along Devon Avenue, where sari shops and Pakistani and Indian restaurants abound. Even lifelong Chicagoans can be astonished by their city's ever-changing character. One man whose tradition it is to drive down an old Swedish section of Foster Avenue for Christmas pastries now finds his Swedish deli surrounded by Middle Eastern bakeries and restaurants.

Fittingly in a city of such diversity, the "Father of Chicago" was a black man, fur trader Jean Baptiste Pointe DuSable, who in 1779 built a home near the present site of the Wrigley Building at the mouth of the Chicago River. He established a trading post that served English, French,

The intersection of Clark and Monroe streets was the heart of downtown in the 1850s, but nothing like the sea of skyscrapers inside the Loop today. In those days before massive landfilling, this was three blocks from Lake Michigan.

The Illinois Central train terminal can be seen from the Michigan Avenue breakwater in the 1800s. Several railroads reaching into the farm belt helped turn Chicago into the Midwest's dominant metropolis.

and Indians alike and brokered peace among neighboring Great Lakes tribes. His homestead was the site of the area's first wedding, election, recorded birth, and court session. Chicago was the principal destination of "The Great Migration" of blacks from the Jim Crow South, when the mechanization of cotton cultivation pushed more than six million African Americans off the farm and toward the industrial North from 1916 through the 1950s. Chicago would spawn Miles Davis and Duke Ellington; welcome King Oliver and Louis Armstrong from New Orleans; and produce Dr. Daniel Hale Williams, who performed the first successful surgery on the human heart. Oscar DePriest, the first black congressman of the twentieth century, and Carol Mosely Braun, the first black U.S. senator ever, belonged to Chicago, as do Mae Jemison, the first African American in space; and Oprah Winfrey, who helped turn talk television into an American pastime. A great hero of black Chicago was charismatic Mayor Harold Washington, who built a remarkable coalition among African Americans, Hispanics, and many whites in the 1980s. And a hero to *all* Chicagoans—at least on the North Side—was baseball star Ernie Banks. Ever smiling, "Mr. Cub" made famous the expression "Let's play two!" whether the Cubbies won or lost.

Jean Baptiste DuSable had been preceded to the southwest corner of Lake Michigan by the Potawatomis and other Native American tribes, none of whom cared to stay in the muddy slough between the lake and the Illinois River. They did, however, use the area, which they called *Chicagoua*, as a portage for their canoes. Some scholars have translated Chicagoua to mean "strong" (for it certainly took great power to lug canoes one hundred miles through the muck); others think it means something less ennobling: "skunkweed," for the profusion of wild onions nearby.

French-Canadian fur trader Louis Joliet and Jesuit missionary Jacques Marquette together visited Chicagoua in 1673, but they did not stay. Neither did the explorer René-Robert Cavelier, Sieur de La Salle, who passed through nine years later on his way to the Mississippi River. In 1763, France ceded the region to Britain as part of the penalty for losing the Seven Years' War, and the British themselves surrendered dominion when they were defeated in the American Revolutionary War. In 1803 a U.S. Army company under Captain John Whistler—later grandfather to the famous painter—arrived and built Fort Dearborn, just inland from the lake. Indians who were allied with the British at the start of the War of 1812 destroyed the fort and massacred every settler but two women and a trader. The Crown's forces were again dispatched, and the fort was rebuilt, stimulating new growth. In 1830, lots were sold to finance construction of what would become the Illinois and Michigan Canal, connecting the settlement by water with the Mississippi and the West. Three years later the Town of Chicago was incorporated. Its population: 350.

Completion of the westward canal and the first rail line into Chicago in 1848 ensured the city's destiny as a transportation axis, and the population—already past five thousand—quickly tripled. Young Cyrus McCormick was one of the newcomers. He had visited the city's first business convocation, the "River and Harbors Convention," liked his prospects in the burgeoning new city, and moved his tiny reaper factory to town. Perfection of the machine, and the opening of the Union Stock Yards in 1865, intertwined the fortunes of Great Plains farms with those of this emerging metropolis.

Chicago became a convention city again in 1860, when the nascent Republican Party nominated Illinois's Abraham Lincoln for president. The Civil War that followed his election spurred tumultuous growth in population, manufacturing, and food processing. By war's end, the city had eleven railroads and more than three hundred thousand residents, soon served by hoteliers and merchants like Potter Palmer and Marshall Field. By century's end a former traveling salesman, Aaron Montgomery Ward, and a watch merchant, Richard Warren Sears, would separately bring the goods of Chicago to country stores, farmhouses, and city and village homes nationwide through direct catalog sales.

The city's "front yard," a greensward along the lake that now offsets the parade of skyscrapers, grew above one of the most incredible landfill projects in history. Rubble from the terrible 1871 Chicago Fire was tossed wholesale into Lake Michigan, so that Michigan Avenue no longer bordered the lake at all. What resulted was a stunning urban playground that today draws more than sixty-five million picnickers, bathers, chess players, fireworks watchers, and even nocturnal smelt fishermen annually.

What to do with the rubble was the least of people's worries after the Great Fire. For two nights and a day, the blaze had devoured three and a half square miles of a city of wood-frame buildings, jumping streets and the river, killing more than three hundred people, leaving

This view from the big Armour company's headquarters building shows a bustling rail yard. At its stockyard, the meatpacker unloaded thousands of cars full of animals for slaughter each day.

Such an attraction was the headquarters of the Montgomery Ward catalog store that more than three hundred thousand people took the free tour of the building during the World's Columbian Exposition in 1893.

visions of American ingenuity and pristine urban life inspired a City Beautiful movement that would awaken and transform many of the nation's tired, dingy cities. Burnham himself won commissions for monolithic structures like the soaring new Union Station in the nation's capital.

The Exposition ignited a cultural explosion, including the founding of the Chicago Symphony and the city's first opera company. Writers like Eugene Field, Theodore Dreiser, and Carl Sandberg flourished. World War I, Prohibition, and the Great Depression brought disquieting cycles of prosperity, immigration, and crime. In 1933 the city staged another world's fair, this one to celebrate its own centennial. It proved so popular that it was held over a full year. By World War II, Chicago had settled majestically into its role as America's "Second City."

Chicago's rapid resurgence was not trouble-free. Already an ethnic mosaic, the city had become the capital of American anarchism. In 1886, someone threw a bomb into a crowd that police had been dispatched to disperse in Haymarket Square. Seven police were killed and sixty injured—with at least as many civilian casualties—prompting a citywide roundup of socialists, anarchists, and labor agitators.

Eight years later, workers in Pullman, south of Chicago, a sometimes-idyllic company town founded by railroad-car magnate George M. Pullman, went on strike, crippling the nation's passenger-rail service. Pullman had reduced wages but not prices in town. It took federal troops to quash the strike, but such bitter relations remained that, when Pullman died, his family buried him in the dead of night in Graceland Cemetery and ordered his casket covered with tons of concrete to discourage would-be defilers of the gravesite.

Throughout its history, Chicago's politics have been tempestuous. Edward J. Kelly first organized the city's Democratic machine for others, then took the mayor's job himself in 1933 when Anton J. Cermak was killed in Miami by an assassin who had been aiming at President Roosevelt. Kelly served four terms, from 1933 to 1947; and his successor, Richard J. Daley, served six, from 1955 to 1975. The cantankerous Daley, feared for his ability to deliver votes against any aldermanic candidate who displeased him, raised the nation's ire in 1968 when he issued "shoot to kill" orders during racial disturbances, then defended his police force from charges of brutality against youthful demonstrators outside the Democratic National Convention. "As long as I am mayor," he huffed at the convention, "there is going to be law and order in Chicago." Daley perfected the spoils system, passing out plum directorates to his pals. Yet he saw to it that capable technocrats ran the departments' day-to-day operations. The mayor was generally right when he called Chicago the City That Works.

Politics is but one of Chicago's passions, with beer, often backed by a shot of something stronger, and sports being two others. For most of the twentieth century, it seemed that every neighborhood streetcorner was anchored by one or more taverns. Not bars; in Chicago they are taverns, the neighborhood social center. But as many communities gentrified, and the second Mayor Daley—Richard J.'s son Richard M.—looked askance at taverns as undesirable eyesores, their numbers began to diminish. Many gave way to art galleries, boutiques, jewelry shops, tapas bars, and chain restaurants.

No matter the clientele, Chicago's tavern talk quickly turns to the fortunes of the city's many longstanding sports teams. Chicago claims founding franchises in both the National Hockey League and the National Football League. The Black Hawks, named for a legendary Native American who was the last to resist white incursion into northern Illinois, perennially qualify for hockey's play-offs. "Da Bears," as late-night television parodied Chicagoans' lunch-pail pronunciation of the old "Monsters of the Midway" franchise, have sustained a tradition as football's paragon "black-and-blue" team.

Baseball's National League Cubs, formed in 1870, are the oldest professional sports franchise operating in the city of their founding, and the White Sox won the pennant in 1901, the first year the American League was upgraded from a minor to a major league. But Chicago might as well be two distant cities when it comes to the loyalties of its baseball fans. With few exceptions, South Siders cheer for the Sox, and with a mixture of masochism and melancholia, North Siders follow the Cubbies, whose mystique has always revolved around their predictable ineptitude. Perversely, each side of town roots *against* the other's team.

The Chicago Bulls were a National Basketball Association expansion franchise in 1966–67, and their workmanlike teams won critical admiration and a small cadre of fans at the ancient Chicago Stadium. But it was not until the 1990s that the Bulls of acrobatic megastar Michael Jordan and meditative coach Phil Jackson turned the Toddlin' Town into a lather of adoration. Murals of Jordan, Dennis Rodman—a tattooed man of unpredictable hair color—and brooding Scottie Pippin popped up all over town, and it was hard to find a kid or a car without the snorting logo of one of pro basketball's greatest all-time teams.

In Chicago, at least downtown, one is rarely "out of the Loop," the name for the elevated

This steamboat on the Chicago River in 1905 was likely a lake steamer, as the Illinois River, connecting the Chicago and Mississippi rivers, could not handle deep-draft vessels until the 1930s.

This view of the Madison Street Bridge came from a 1909 postcard, sent by a teacher to one of his students back in Massachusetts. The city was already an important tourist destination.

railroad line that has encircled the commercial center since 1893. It's also hard, in many neighborhoods, to *ignore* the El when it rattles past at bedroom-window height. Though the passenger trains of a half dozen railroads no longer converge on Union Station, Metra commuter trains bring in a workforce from Wilmette, Riverside, Elgin, and other outlying towns.

Increasingly Chicago's forever-inadequate ribbon of freeways is clogged in *both* directions at rush hour, as city residents head for work outside town at the same time the crush from suburbia is heading inward. Even cities as far removed as Rockford, ninety miles away, are caught in this urban-to-suburban beat. Chicago is a central hub of the nation's interstate highway system, and thus a natural trucking capital. The interstate crossroads look inviting to transcontinental travelers, but woe unto unsuspecting drivers expecting a speedy journey from Chicago to Wisconsin or Indiana at noon on a summer Friday, or in the other direction on Sunday afternoons. Chicagoans brag about their public transportation but cling tightly to their steering wheels, braving the "Dan Ryan," "Edens," "Stevenson," "Kennedy," and the "Eisenhower" (the city prefers names, not numbers, for its expressways).

While freeways are engineering marvels, it is the achievements of the successors to the Chicago School architects who have kept the city an architectural crucible. To be asked to design a building in Chicago is a high honor, usually bestowed only after a rigorous design competition. Such was the case in the late 1980s when funds were found to build a new central library, to be named for the late Mayor Washington. By January 1988, more than seventy architects, developers, and contractors had formed alliances that created five semifinalist design teams. Visitors to the city cultural center were invited to review the teams' models and make suggestions, and a jury of eleven civil, business, and architectural leaders picked the "SEBUS Group" as the winner.

The looming red-stone structure, which immediately became the world's largest public library, has the look of the eighteenth century. Underneath its owl-like gargoyles are almost nine million books and other pieces, yet the city does not expect to fill the seventy miles of shelving until the fourth decade of the new millenium. The library's collections include works of Chicago authors and about Chicago history, theater, and art, and the Civil War effects of Illinois men and women who served in the Union Army. Some of the library's reading alcoves reach two stories, and a ninth-floor winter garden rises fifty-two feet above the benches and greenery.

Chicago's oldest cultural institution, the Chicago Historical Society, is noted for its American History Wing and its exhibit and film on the Great Chicago Fire. Until it began charging admission in 1991, the Museum of Science and Industry was the second-most-visited museum in America, behind Washington's Air and Space Museum. Visitors can tour the actual *Apollo 8* capsule, a captured World War II German U-505 submarine, and take a ride on the "Augernaut" to the "center of the earth."

Over the first three decades of the twentieth century, Chicago welcomed an array of other attractions that cemented its standing as a world-class city: the John G. Shedd Aquarium—still the world's largest such facility—was the gift of the president and board chairman of Marshall Field & Co. department store. Live sharks, sea turtles, and tropical fish populate the aquarium; and sea otters, whales, dolphins, and seals live in the 1990 Oceanarium annex. Graham, Anderson, Probst & White's 1930 structure itself incorporates crabs, lobsters, waves, and shells into the façade. The Field Museum, moved to a building inspired by a Greek temple in Burnham Park in 1921, was endowed by Marshall Field I. Its dinosaur exhibit is dominated by a seventy-two-foot-long Apatosaurus, the "Traveling the Pacific" permanent exhibition duplicates the lava flow of an active Hawaiian volcano, the wonders of Pharaoh Unis-ankh's tomb are revealed, and children are invited to handle skeletons, meteorites, and other objects in the "Place of Wonder." Like the Smithsonian's Museum of Natural History in Washington, the Field Museum reserves ninety-nine percent of its holdings for scientific study, out of public view. Adler Planetarium, funded by Sears, Roebuck & Company executive Max Adler, offers sky shows in the domed theater, and a peek at the nighttime sky through the Doane Observatory, as well as a terrestrial look at the city skyline from the planetarium's promontory.

The 1892 Art Institute of Chicago, whose bronze lions outside the South Michigan Avenue entrance have become the institute's symbol and a favorite city landmark, was timed for completion just ahead of the Columbian Exposition, as a showcase for the city's proud cultural treasures. Today one of America's four largest art museums, with a collection valued at more than $250 million, it houses a stunning collection of French Impressionist and Postimpressionist paintings. Visitors are eternally fascinated by the institute's miniature rooms, detailing replicas of mansions and other buildings, some less than an inch high. At Christmas, the sentinel lions are girded in wreaths, and they have been known to sport Cubs hats, Bears helmets, and other sporting paraphernalia when the city's teams reach an important game. In 1996, the Museum of Contemporary Art got a new $46-million home, including a sculpture garden, in the shadow of the old Water Tower near the lakefront. Architect Josef Paul Kleihues's 125,000-foot building, which houses a more modernist art collection, including ties, clocks, artists'

Grant Park, on the doorstep of downtown Chicago, was one of many oases of green in Daniel Burnham's 1909 Chicago Plan that reserved the city's "front yard" for recreation and contemplation.

books, abstract paintings, and even T-shirts, was constructed on space previously occupied by the Chicago Avenue Armory. At the "MCA," even the grand staircase, which Kleihues likened to the propylaea of the Acropolis and the steps of the Altes Museum in Berlin, are art.

Chicago is also home to delightfully different galleries and exhibitions. The DuSable Museum of African American History offers performances of music and dance and a "know your heritage" quiz. The Oriental Institute Museum at the University of Chicago features a monumental statue of Pharaoh Tutankhamen and a forty-ton winged Assyrian bull-man relief among its five galleries of artifacts from the ancient Near East. The city also contains the Polish Museum of America, the nation's largest Mexican museum, the Balzekas Museum of Lithuanian Culture, the Swedish-American Museum Center, and the Ukrainian National Museum. Visitors with even more eclectic interests can find the International Museum of Surgical Science, with an extensive collection of early microscopes, x-ray equipment, and displays about acupuncture; the Museum of Contemporary Photography; the Museum of Broadcast Communications; the Museum of Holography, filled with three-dimensional laser images; the Terra Museum devoted to American art; and a Museum of Floral Arts. There's the May Weber Museum of Cultural Arts, which displays puppets, ceremonial shawls, and even a teeth-blackening tray; the Ling Long Museum of ethnic Chinese culture and art; a bicycle museum and virtual-reality "digital theme park" at the North Pier shopping arcade in a converted furniture warehouse; and two museums of Judaica.

A summer magnet is the Ferris wheel at the three-thousand-foot-long Navy Pier, built in 1916 for commercial shipping. And historic buildings like Union Station, the old Chicago & Northwestern train terminal, the Sun-Times Building, the Water Tower, and Tribune Tower are open to visitors. The Water Tower, in fact, is one nexus of the city's visitor-information services,

By the 1920s, Michigan Avenue was well established as the commercial spine of Chicago. This view southward from Chicago Avenue shows the results of the city's careful planning and eye for beauty.

offering maps and brochures in several languages. Chicago loves to compile unusual facts and statistics. A visitor can learn, for instance, that the city boasts fifty movable bridges and produced the first roller skates (1884), Cracker Jacks (1893), zipper (1896), envelopes with windows (1902), Hostess Twinkie (1930), pinball game (1930), spray paint (sometime in the late 1940s), and McDonald's "Golden Arches" (1955). Chicago even keeps track of the number of billions of Oreo cookies turned out by Nabisco at the world's largest cookie and cracker factory.

Union Station, which replaced the 1881 Pennsylvania Railroad Station, was the last of Daniel Burnham's train-terminal projects. He died before construction was completed in 1925; the project, passed on to the firm of Graham, Anderson, Probst and White, had been interrupted by World War I and took ten years to complete. Clad in Bedford limestone quarried in Indiana, Chicago Union Station is the only U.S. railroad station with a "double-stub" track layout. Metra commuter and Amtrak long-distance passenger trains approach the station from two directions, with most tracks dead-ending at the concourse. The grand staircase in the renovated and mechanically upgraded terminal was prominently featured in a bloody shootout between mob characters and the forces of the G-man Elliot Ness in the 1987 movie *The Untouchables*.

The Merchandise Mart, another protean structure, remains the world's largest commercial building. Built by Marshall Field in 1931 to house showrooms and offices for wholesale dealers of giftware, office furnishings, and business products—it was sold to Joseph P. Kennedy during the Depression. The mart encloses more than four million square feet, employs more than nine thousand people, and draws more than ten thousand tradespeople a day. Its trade floors are open only to dealers, architects, and designers, but the first two floors have been converted into a retail mall.

In the 1940s the Navy Pier at the mouth of the Chicago River was the world's largest "commercial and pleasure pier," with shopping promenades and an inspiring view of the Chicago skyline.

167—Outer Drive Link Bridge and Skyline, Chicago

The Outer Drive Link Bridge, shown here in 1951, connected north and south Chicago and opened a pleasant route along the lakefront to the Lincoln Park Zoo, the northern suburbs, and beyond.

Perhaps no other spot in Chicago epitomizes the city's openness and accessibility better than Lincoln Park. Situated on 1,208 acres of lakefront, reclaimed from Lake Michigan in the 1860s, the park includes one of the last free zoos in America. Lincoln Park Zoo is noted for its ape house, rookery, the adjacent three acres of greenhouses known as the Lincoln Park Conservatory, and a separate "Farm-in-the-Zoo," a five-acre replica of a Midwest farm. The parkland also includes the North Avenue bathing beach; North and South ponds, which are festooned with paddleboats in summer and ice skaters in winter; a chess pavilion; a bike and in-line skating path; a golf course; and a driving range.

There's not a lot of "old money" in vibrant Chicago, by the standards of some cities, but there are monuments to wealth, nonetheless. One is the Gold Coast neighborhood, where power brokers, business leaders, and the city's Roman Catholic archbishop live in weathered mansions or exclusive high-rise apartment buildings. The neighborhood was born in 1882, when Potter Palmer, founder of the Palmer House—which would become Chicago's oldest hotel—filled in a frog pond on Lake Shore Drive and built what he called a "mansion to end all mansions." Over the next fifty years, other urban castles, several deluxe apartment buildings, and the opulent Drake Hotel followed. Palmer's own hotel, which became a Hilton in 1945, opened on the corner of State and Quincy streets in the Loop on September 26, 1871. Thirteen days later, the Great Fire burned it to the ground. It was immediately rebuilt for a staggering $3.5 million. In 1925, the hotel was demolished in two sections and replaced, half at a time, by the current hotel. That year, the hotel opened the sumptuous Empire Room supper club, which featured its own troupe of dancers and helped launch Liberace, Maurice Chevalier, Carol Channing, Tony Bennett, and other entertainers to stardom.

Chicago's elite are catered to at many members-only clubs, including the Union League Club,

Woman's Athletic Club, Racquet Club, the Casino, the Chicago Club, and the Saddle & Cycle Club. Some offer the cigar-friendly bars and reading rooms full of overstuffed chairs that are cartoonists' fodder. Private clubs continue to serve as fashionable residences, an in-town base for powerful members who have moved to the suburbs, and a place above the day's din to meet, have lunch, and do deals. With four financial exchanges—the Chicago Board of Trade, the Chicago Mercantile Exchange, the Chicago Stock Exchange, and the Chicago Board Options Exchange—huge public companies like Amoco, Sara Lee, Quaker Oats, and Inland Steel, and numerous privately held corporations headquartered in town, there are plenty of deals to be done.

There is another, far more vibrant "club scene" of course. *Chicago Magazine* and Chicago's free newspaper, called simply *Reader*, devote long sections to nightspots with intriguing names, from Alcatrazz, Elbo Room, Set 'Em Up Joe, Smart Bar, and Empty Bottle, to Crobar, Dick's Last Resort, Hoghead McDunna's, and the Bourgeois Pig Coffee House. And those are just the rock bars. Folk, country, blues, gospel, jazz, and even Korean percussion, flamenco guitar, Greek music, and players of instruments called the klezmer and the cimbalom have regular followings in lively Chicago.

Midwesterners have long made an expedition out of shopping in the big State Street department stores and off-price retailers, and at swankier shops along North Michigan Avenue. Its "Magnificent Mile" includes three "vertical shopping malls" containing more than two hundred shops, restaurants, and cinemas. And neighborhood streets like Clark, Lincoln, and Broadway have become packed with boutiques, flea markets, and bookstores alongside cozy cafés. Even the City of Chicago has a store in North Pier, peddling not just city banners, posters, and street signs, but also authentic ballot boxes, parking meters, and manhole covers. What better evidence could there be that sprawling Chicago is approachable, open to new ideas, and eager to please?

Bustling, hard-working Chicago in the 1950s was America's undisputed No. 2 city. Its administration was in the firm grip of Mayor Richard J. Daley's Democratic political machine.

South Michigan Avenue (left) offers one architectural treat after another. An automobile journey here is often speedy, in contrast to the slow going on the cross streets of the Loop. ABOVE: In the city's central core, Michigan Avenue winds around the stately Wrigley Building as it crosses the Chicago River.

PRECEDING PAGES: The boxy, rust-colored building in the foreground is the CNA Building, whose drab color turns vivid at sunset. The structure with the distinctive angled, diamond-shaped face—the Stone Container Building—was the first office tower in Chicago to be wired for computers.

The Old Colony Building (above) on South Dearborn Street at West Van Buren is a downtown landmark. RIGHT: Daniel Burnham's 1910 Peoples Gas Building on South Michigan Avenue was a state-of-the-art office tower, with imported mahogany, Greek marble, a light court graced with Tiffany glass, and fourteen passenger elevators. It offered valet service, manicure rooms, showers, safe-deposit boxes, and a public stenographer. OVERLEAF: Burnham's imaginative but less flamboyant partner John Wellborn Root designed the Rookery Building in the city's financial district. This stairway rises from the building's dynamic central light court—a starburst of marble, glazed brick, translucent glass, and serpentine stairs remindful of London's Crystal Palace of 1851.

Along with traditional German dishes, Berghoff's, a Chicago institution, offers its private-label beer and bourbon. In fact, the restaurant holds Chicago liquor license No. 1. During Prohibition, Berghoff's served near beer and "Bergo Soda Pop."
LEFT TOP: One of the city's best-loved and most meticulously restored downtown structures is the Monadnock Building, designed by Burnham and Root in 1889 and nearly doubled in size by Holabird and Roche in 1893. Because the building is all masonry, with no steel skeleton, its walls are six feet thick at the base.
BOTTOM: The prolific Burnham also designed Marshall Field's & Co.'s signature State Street store. Its founder coined the maxim "Give the lady what she wants!" Field's has restored the downtown store to its early splendor and opened several branches.

The "People's Palace"—the 1897 Chicago Cultural Center—includes a rotunda dedicated to the Grand Army of the Republic. Its intricate Renaissance-pattern stained-glass dome was executed by the studio of Healy and Millet. Another wing features what's thought to be the world's largest Tiffany dome. Originally the city's main library building, the "Palace" offers free artistic programs and exhibits and houses the city's official visitor information center.

RIGHT: Edward Kerneys' guardian lions in front of the Art Institute of Chicago are familiar and occasionally whimsical landmarks, sometimes outfitted in a local sports team's paraphernalia before an important game.

OVERLEAF: Ariste Maillol Frene's bronze sculpture Chained Action dominates the institute's central hall. An early elevator grille from the Chicago Stock Exchange is among the items displayed above.

The ubiquitous Daniel Burnham designed the one-million-square-foot home of the Field Museum of Natural History in Grant Park. Named for the museum's chief benefactor, Marshall Field I, the museum added two of the largest living land animals, two fighting bull elephants (left) in 1905 and 1906. ABOVE: The bones of Albertosaurus, a smaller cousin to the ferocious Tyran-nosaurus, *stand in the museum's Halls of Life Over Time. The Field Museum includes encyclopedic collections of more than twenty million specimens, extensive laboratories and libraries, and a* community of scholars studying biology and anthropology throughout the world. The museum was first housed in the World's Columbian Exposition's Palace of Fine Arts. A plaster structure, it crumbled over the years, necessitating the move to a new neoclassical building on city parkland. Beginning in 1984, the Field Museum undertook a massive $40-million renovation.

Chicago's glorious City Hall, whose spacious marble hallways are usually teeming with citizens who have business with the city, was designed by Holabird and Roche. The building also houses Cook County's offices. OPPOSITE: Chicago's $75-million Union Station, clad in Indiana limestone, was completed in 1925. The station, which replaced an old Pennsylvania Railroad terminal in 1911, is the nation's third-busiest. Its headhouse includes an eight-story office building and the waiting room for Metra commuter and Amtrak long-distance trains. Almost one hundred thousand commuters pass through the terminal on an average weekday. A concourse building that stood above the tracks between Canal Street and the Chicago River was demolished in 1969 to make way for the Gateway III office building. An extensive renovation added air-conditioning, brighter lighting, and improved heating and fire-protection systems to the old station.

The Chicago Theater, in Chicago's Loop, defined elegance when it opened in 1921. The "Wonder Theatre of the World" was a veritable palais, replete with crystal chandeliers and fabulous objets d'art, including cloisonné vases and Carrara busts. By 1982 it was all but abandoned and set for demolition. Rescued by new owners and the Illinois Landmarks Preservation Council, the theater got a beautiful facelift—including a "re-moisturizing" of its magnificent murals. ABOVE: This and an identical statue were executed by Michelangelo Studios of Chicago, which had supplied the statues to the 1893 Chicago World's Fair.

The Chapel in the Sky is located four hundred feet high in the stone spire of the Chicago Temple (the First United Methodist Church). First used on Easter morning in 1952, the sky chapel was the gift of Mrs. Charles R. Walgreen in memory of her husband, founder of the Walgreen drugstore chain. Below a Greek cross in the ceiling is Jerome Walters's illuminated woodcarving of Jesus, looking northeast over the city of Chicago. It is a companion piece to an Alois Lang altar carving in the sanctuary, depicting Christ seated on the Mount of Olives. The church's "Upper Room" is used for weddings, baptisms, communion services, and other occasions. ABOVE: This window inset depicts the church's building that burned to the ground in the Great Chicago Fire of 1871.

Graham, Anderson, and Probst designed both the John G. Shedd Aquarium (left) in 1929 and the Merchandise Mart (above) in 1930. The Shedd Aquarium offers winding nature trails through a re-created Pacific Northwest coastline, an Asian river exhibit, several examples of coral reefs, and even a Caribbean iguana habitat. The aquarium asks visitors to "water your imagination" by observing more than eight thousand animals representing more than 650 species. The Merchandise Mart is the world's largest wholesalers' building. Most dealers specialize in interior design. The first two floors are now a retail shopping mall, anchored by a branch of Carson Pirie Scott department store. The row of busts, depicting notable merchants, was added in front of the building in 1953 at the behest of owner Joseph P. Kennedy, patriarch of the famous "Kennedy Clan." Shown are, right to left, Marshall Field, Frank Winfield Woolworth, and Julius Rosenwald.

More than any other American city, Chicago is an outdoor sculpture gallery. In 1967 when it appeared on a plaza on Washington Street, "The Picasso," as it is known—the Spanish artist's fifty-foot abstract, untitled steel creation—immediately became Chicago's Eiffel Tower, a symbol of the vibrant city. Other modern sculptures, including a giant steel baseball bat; an aluminum creation called Splash; *a painted aluminum wall called* Lines in Four Directions; *and* Big Beaver, *a "contemporary totem pole," would follow.*

OPPOSITE: *For decades, the Quaker Oats Company maintained its world headquarters in the Merchandise Mart, before moving into its own glass-skin building along the Chicago River in 1991. Two giant replicas of the company's most famous product adorn the lobby of the building, designed by Skidmore, Owings & Merrill.*

Nearly everyone who spoke at the dedication of the Harold Washington Library Center in the South Loop in 1991 noted that the late Chicago mayor loved to read. The building blended uncannily with turn-of-the-century neighbors like the Old Colony Building and the city auditorium. The monolith immediately became the world's largest public library. ABOVE: Outdoor exhibitions of bronze sculptures in Grant Park, placed in early May and removed in late October, have become a Chicago tradition. The Department of Cultural Affairs has acquired, and creatively displayed, a vast public art collection. OVERLEAF: Chicago's reputation as the "Windy City" is earned, especially on East Wacker Drive along the river, even if the nickname actually resulted from the verbal windiness of the promoters of its world's fair.

CITY · OF · CHICAGO ·

HENRY HERING SC.

DEFENSE

FORT DEARBORN STOOD ALMOST ON THIS SPOT.
AFTER AN HEROIC DEFENSE IN EIGHTEEN
HUNDRED AND TWELVE, THE GARRISON TOGETHER
WITH WOMEN AND CHILDREN WAS FORCED TO EVACUATE
THE FORT. LED FORTH BY CAPTAIN WELLS, THEY
WERE BRUTALLY MASSACRED BY THE INDIANS.
THEY WILL BE CHERISHED AS MARTYRS IN
OUR EARLY HISTORY

ERECTED BY THE TRUSTEES OF THE
B. F. FERGUSON MONUMENT FUND
1928

OPPOSITE: *Edward Bennett designed the Defense relief on the Michigan Avenue Bridge in 1920. It commemorates the determination to rebuild Fort Dearborn on this site after Indians allied with British forces destroyed the fort and massacred most of its settlers during the War of 1812.* LEFT: *Chicago's beloved 1866 Water Tower, designed by William Boyington, anchors a lovely park on North Michigan Avenue. Horse-drawn carriages assemble around it, and the city maintains a visitor-information center there. The tower was part of an elaborate system in which water was pulled through tunnels from Lake Michigan and sent to a pumping station across the street. It was then pumped into the water tower, which helped equalize pressure so the water could be distributed to municipal water mains.*

55

The penthouse of the Executive Plaza Hotel offers an unusual view of movable bridges over the Chicago River, looking northwest toward Wolf Point. The "twin corncob" Marina City apartments were designed by Bertrand Goldberg from 1959 to 1967. To the river's left runs Wacker Drive, the nation's only downtown street that turns hard north, east, south, and west. ABOVE: The brilliantly lit, 1919 Wrigley Building, famous for its wedding-cake embellishments and clock tower, was long a symbol of dynamic Chicago. OVERLEAF: Navy Pier's Ferris wheel offers an animated perspective of the city skyline.

1897 Old Hickory

Tonk Manufacturing Co.,
Chicago

Tonk, like some other manufacturers, thought wood would be good for frames because it absorbed vibrations better than steel. Whether it had a smooth ride or not, the Old Hickory was beautiful, with its spare design and ornamental lugs.

On loan from Schwinn Development Co.

The Bicycle Museum of America is one attraction at North Pier, an indoor shopping arcade in a converted warehouse on East Illinois Street. The museum offers a panoply of bikes, from early models to today's most sophisticated racing cycles. It sponsors long-distance bike tours and offers historical exhibits, such as the history of women in cycling. ABOVE: Most visitors enter the Museum of Contemporary Art building, which opened on East Chicago Avenue in 1996, on a grand staircase that is itself modern art. The building's German architect, Joseph Paul Kleihues, likens the stairway to the propylaea of the Acropolis and the steps of the Altes Museum in Berlin. The museum and its sculpture garden, which were Kleihues's first U.S. project, rose in the shadow of the city's historic Water Tower on a site formerly occupied by a National Guard armory.

Simple but delicious food is a Chicago obsession. Sports fans love the chumminess of the Billy Goat Tavern underneath the Chicago River Bridge. The restaurant was founded by William Sianis in 1934. He served goat cheese along with his burgers and fried onions, and newspaper writers took to calling him "The Goat." BOTTOM: A Chicago creation is deep-dish pizza, which Gino's East on Superior Street has been baking for more than thirty years. Founded by two cabdrivers, Gino's has a taxi motif, and customers are invited to add tasteful graffiti to most of the restaurant's walls. OPPOSITE: Harry Caray, the legendary Cubs baseball announcer, opened a restaurant in a historic building, designed by Henry Ives Cobb in 1900, on West Kinzie Street. Caray's beloved "Cubbies" often drop by.

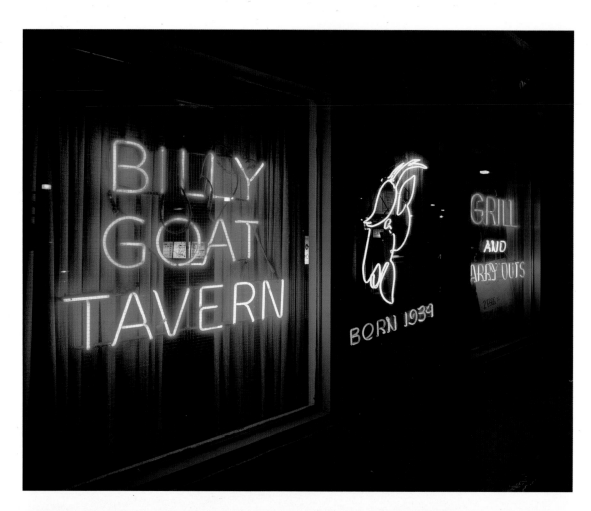

The Gold Coast, long one of Chicago's most fashionable neighborhoods, is replete with elegant brownstone mansions and apartment buildings. The neighborhood was the creation of Potter Palmer, owner of the Palmer House Hotel. In the 1880s, he bought a stretch of marsh and dunes along Lake Michigan north of town, added lake-bottom sand as landfill, and invited his friends to join him in building stately manors there. At his own castle Potter's wife, Bertha, became Chicago's most famous hostess; the English dining room seated fifty, and the rooftop ballroom was the site of the city's most lavish parties. The city facilitated travel to and from the Potters' soirees by constructing a road, later called Lake Shore Drive, up to the Gold Coast.

Dearborn Parkway (right), south of Lincoln Park, is one of the most refined of Gold Coast avenues. Apartment towers and low-rise office buildings have been tastefully integrated into the neighborhood of turreted brownstones. OPPOSITE: The Second City Comedy Club occupies a beautiful old building on North Wells Street. The legendary improvisational club was the training ground for comedians like Elaine May, Joan Rivers, John Belushi, Bill Murray, and Shelly Long. It spawned several branches, including one in Toronto that produced Dan Akroyd and John Candy. Chicago is also home to a half-dozen other comedy clubs, as well as myriad jazz, dance, blues, and country-music clubs, as well as eclectic nightspots featuring everything from sambas to zither music.

The Lincoln Park Zoo (above), the nation's oldest zoological park, began in 1868 with the gift of a pair of swans. Now more than one thousand animals are exhibited. The zoo is an enthusiastic participant in "SSPs"— species survival plans, established by the American Zoo and Aquarium Association, designed to ensure the continued genetic diversity of animals in captivity throughout North America. The Lincoln Park Conservatory (right), north of the zoo, features palm, fern, and cactus houses. It mounts enormously popular azalea shows in February, Easter shows in March or April, crysthanthemum shows in November, and a lavish Christmas show in December. Lincoln Park is a testament to architectural ingenuity, as most of the park and its nearby residential neighborhood were underwater prior to 1860.

Recreation along Lake Michigan's North Avenue Beach is both active and sedentary. Cyclists, in-line skaters, joggers, and skateboarders whiz past the Lincoln Park Chess Pavilion, which seems to attract players even on cool and misty days. Carved king and queen figures on each end of the 1950s-vintage pavilion inspire players. A spring ritual along the lakefront is the harvesting of smelt. Fishers—often whole families out for a nighttime diversion— attract the spawning creatures at night using small lights, and the shoreline during smelt season looks like a necklace of Chinese lanterns. ABOVE: Few other northern cities can offer so pleasant and expansive a beachfront as Chicago. But only the hardy brave the icy winds that swirl on the lakefront in winter.

Many cities across the nation have enlisted the help of developers to turn harbors or other sections into festival marketplaces, parkland, or recreation districts in order to add life to downtown. But no such efforts are needed in Chicago, which has a ready-made playland on its beaches, bike paths, parks, and out on Lake Michigan itself. Weekdays, weekends, and even many evenings, there's family activity on the beach (above and right). Chicago's twenty miles of beaches are open to swimmers from morning to sunset during months when the water temperature is bearable, and some even have changing facilities. Beachgoers have a busy scene in front of them in the harbor (overleaf), and those who are out on the water enjoy a spectacular view of the Chicago skyline.

The fishing is fine at several spots along the lake (above). Perch, catfish, and trout are commonly caught, but there's an occasional salmon to be snagged as well. Tackle ranges from a simple line dropped off a pier to sophisticated casting rods that fling tempting morsels out into deep water. Those who keep their sailboats in the harbor can catch a lift to their boats from the Department of Recreation, which keeps its own boats at the dock (right). And the lakefront is home to some of the finest yachts on the Great Lakes (opposite). Sailboat lessons and rentals are available at several locations, though newcomers are advised that winds, shoals, and rocks along the shoreline can be tricky and sometimes treacherous.

The Lake Shore Drive Synagogue (opposite), built in the late 1800s in Lincoln Park, is one of the city's most beautiful houses of worship. ABOVE: A specter stands before the tomb of Chicago pioneer Dexter Graves in Graceland Cemetery on the city's North Side. Graves brought thirteen families to Chicago aboard a schooner from Ashtabula, Ohio, in 1831. Many nineteenth-century luminaries, including George Pullman, Louis Sullivan, and Marshall Field, are buried in this cemetery. OVERLEAF: Wrigley Field, home of North Siders' lovable Cubs, is an old-fashioned, intimate setting for a baseball game. The "friendly confines" of the park produce a procession of home runs when the wind is blowing out from home plate. Baseball purists lost a battle when this last remaining major-league stadium without lights added them in 1988 and began playing night as well as day games.

COFFEE ☕ CHICAGO

With student help, Lane Technical High School teacher Patrick Dawson sculpted— and teacher Ted Szalinski painted— this totem, Ignorance to Wisdom, *for the school's golden jubilee* in 1983. The highly selective school has more than four thousand students. ABOVE: *Three locations of Coffee Chicago, including this one in an elegant old office building, can be* found on eclectic Clark Street, which has become a haven of offbeat antique stores, art studios, cafés, and coffee bars. OVERLEAF: *The price is right at the McDonald's Museum, an actual* McDonald's location from the 1950s—when "only" a million or so McDonald's burgers had been sold— preserved in the suburb of Des Plaines. Vintage cars, a menu from the period, and figures in crisp white uniforms of the times welcome visitors. The company's arches are familiar, though the character holding the price sign has disappeared from company advertising.

Evanston boasts a thriving historical society, located in the Charles Gates Dawes House, the châteauesque mansion of the Nobel laureate. Designed in 1894 for Northwestern University's treasurer by New York architect Henry Edwards-Ficken, it was purchased as a retreat by Dawes sixteen years before he became Calvin Coolidge's vice-president. LEFT: The 1873 Grosse Point Light Station, which once warned ships away from Lake Michigan's rocky shores, stands behind the Evanston Art Center. Now inactive as a lighthouse, the structure is a nature and maritime center, bypassed by a wildflower trail. ABOVE: Ravinia Park in suburban Glencoe hosts a summer music festival and other outdoor entertainment. OVERLEAF: O'Hare International Airport is a classic hub, both of airlines and of twenty-four-hour activity.

Oak Park (left and above), west of downtown Chicago, contains the world's largest collection of Prairie School buildings, which have been designated as a National Historic District. The Prairie style, created by Frank Lloyd Wright, who built a house (overleaf) in Oak Park, was noteworthy for its flowing, horizontal lines that seemed to fit the expansive Great Plains. In 1889 at age twenty-two, Wright borrowed $5,000 from his mentor Louis Sullivan and built his wood-shingle home. Oak Park also features Ernest Hemingway's birthplace and a separate Hemingway museum; the stark, concrete Unity Temple, designed by Wright and built by Unitarians in 1905; a conservatory; and a children's museum.

In his home, Frank Lloyd Wright was true to his architectural beliefs. Both his drafting room (right) and family playroom (opposite) reflect his penchant for simplicity of form and function. Wright, who raised six children with his first wife, Catherine (before leaving her for the wife of a client), experimented with styles and materials here. Five years after building the house in 1893, he added a professional studio, where he completed one quarter of his life's work. This included the Robie House in Chicago, his masterpiece of horizontal planes, cantilevers and ribbons of glass windows that he copied in smaller scale in homes built for clients across America. The Wright Home and Studio is now owned by the National Trust for Historic Preservation.

The Garfield Park Conservatory (above and opposite) is one of the world's largest greenhouses. Built in what was once called Central Park, it was created in 1906–07 as a work of land-scape art under glass by Prairie School landscape architect Jens Jensen, with help from architects and engineers. Inspired by "the great haystacks which are so eloquent of the richness of prairie soil," Jensen replaced a series of small greenhouses with one gigantic facility. It includes a large palm house, a stunning fern room, a lagoon, and a "prairie water-fall." OVERLEAF: Metra commuter trains pass under the Des Plaines Avenue overpass as they chug westward toward Elgin. The curving, modernist structure to the right is the 333 West Wacker Drive Building. The shim-mering green-glass building, designed by Kohn Pedersen Fox in 1983, follows the curve of the Chicago River below.

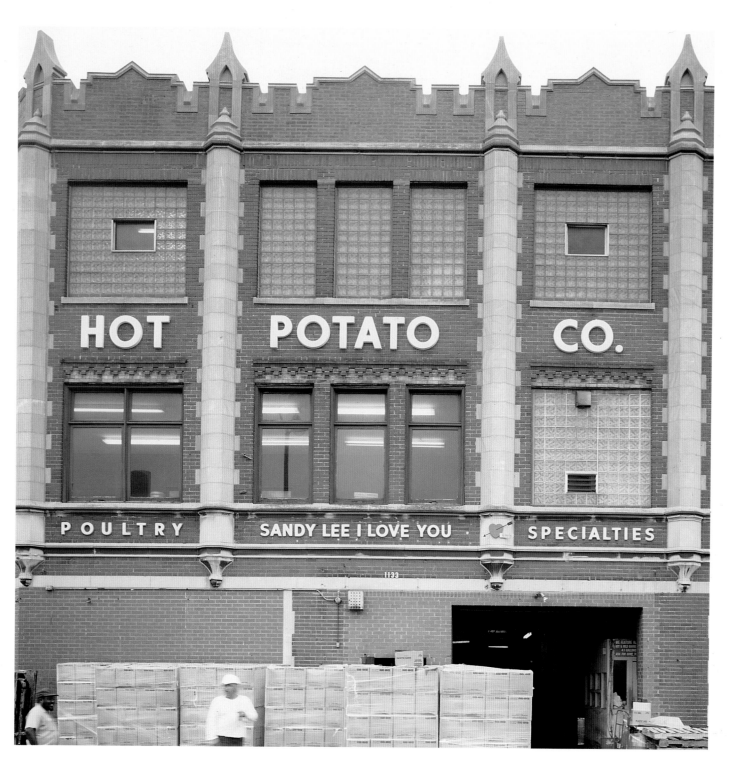

Chicago's unpredictable array of small businesses inspires double-takes and chuckles through clever signage and advertising. The All Ways Ink Tattoo Parlor (opposite) is located on Milwaukee Avenue; the Hot Potato Company (above), with its baffling "Sandy Lee I Love You" inscription above the door, and the lavishly designed Chicago Importing Company (overleaf) are on West Randolph Street. On these thoroughfares, and on Clark and Halsted streets, Clybourn and Broadway avenues, and Diversey Parkway, merchants seem to vie for the cleverest slogans and most creative outdoor designs, matching the sometimes-whimsical merchandise inside. Shoppers who prefer chain and outlet stores can find them mixed in with these unconventional emporiums. Add the ethnic flavor of the city's innumerable delis, bakeries, taverns, and corner restaurants, and you are confronted with an almost impossible choice of where to begin.

The "Mural of Heroes" (above), designed by an unidentified 14th District police officer, adorns the side of a Milwaukee Avenue bank building in the Diversey neighborhood. Its words read, "Our modern day hero is still and always will be those who are brave enough to risk their lives in order that another be saved." RIGHT: There is no question who is Chicago's recent, and perhaps all-time, sports hero. Superstar Michael Jordan, depicted in this Owen Wong painting on the side of a Chicago building, captured the city's heart with his prolific scoring and amazing moves on a basketball court, and with his wink and cheerful disposition. His presence in the lineup made a Bulls game— in opposing arenas as well as Chicago's United Center— the toughest ticket in pro basketball.

Chicago's Chinatown (top) south of downtown is compact. It is largely confined to South Wentworth Avenue but is loaded with gustatory gems. BOTTOM: Like deep-dish pizza, the hot dog is a Chicago artform, and it is prepared with panache (and any number of garnishes) at the Superdawg, a quirky drive-in on North Milwaukee Avenue. Further north of the city, as one nears the Wisconsin border, the influence of the bratwurst (as in a "brat and a beer") begins to be felt, but Chicago is old-fashioned frankfurter country. OPPOSITE: Mario's, on West Taylor Street, restricts its lemonade-making to the warm months.

MARIO'S
ITALIAN LEMONADE

SNOW
SEEDS+
LUPI

SNOWBALL
Flavors

LEMON
VANILLA
ROOT BEER
COCONUT
ORANGE
STRAWBERRY
BLUE RASP.
PINEAPPLE
GRAPE
BANANA
CHERRY
LIME
BLACK CHERRY

PLEASE, HELP KEEP
OUR NEIGHBORHOOD
CLEAN.
PLACE TRASH
IN TRASH CANS

ICE COLD
DRINKING
LEMONADE
1.00 and up

TIP
JAR
Thanks!

LEMONADE
Flavors

LEMON
WATERMELON
BANANA
CHERRY
LIME
STRAWBERRY
BLUE RASPBERRY
ORANGE
CHOCOLATE
PINEAPPLE
COCONUT
CANTALOPE
GRAPE
PIÑA COLADA

Every summer in Chicago, there is a colossal mass food-sampling called the "Taste of Chicago." Even presidents of the United States have stopped by to sample the incredible assortment of ethnic and traditional American cuisine. But Chicagoans and visitors can avoid the crowds by simply hopping in their cars and driving along the city's main arteries, where the assortment of culinary options seems never-ending. The Polish influence is still strong in old Chicago, for instance, and bakeries like the Pasieka (right) on North Milwaukee Avenue, and restaurants such as the Busy Bee (above) on North Damen Avenue, offer delights fit for Warsaw. Notable at the Busy Bee are the czarina (duck gravy soup) and pierogis stuffed with meat and potatoes or potato and sauerkraut.

Among the displays at the Polish Museum of America (above) on North Milwaukee Avenue is the re-created New York hotel room where incomparable pianist Ignaczi Paderewski lived and practiced his craft. The museum collects materials on the lives of Poles in America, including Revolutionary War hero Tadeusz Koscziusko. It also displays the Stations of the Cross from the first Polish church in America, which, curiously, was in Texas. Multiethnic Chicago also houses many other ethnic cultural centers, including the Balzekas Museum of Lithuanian Culture, the DuSable Museum of African American History, the Mexican Fine Arts Center, the Oriental Institute, the Swedish-American Museum, and the Ukrainian Institute of Modern Art.

OPPOSITE: A variety of tongues can be heard in the city's churches, synagogues, and mosques as well. Holy Trinity Catholic Church, for instance, holds services in Polish.

The Minnekirken Norwegian Lutheran Memorial Church on Logan Square was built in 1908. OPPOSITE: The owners of the Salvage One warehouse search the world for architectural remnants that are now prized additions to restored homes and gardens. Normally a historic city would provide an ample supply, but much of Chicago was literally turned to rubble that was used for Lake Michigan landfill after the catastrophic Great Fire of 1871. OVERLEAF: In 1875, Burnham and Root architects designed the stone gate to the great Union Stock Yard. It, and a nondescript industrial park, stand where pens and slaughterhouses once filled 475 acres of South Chicago.

The Historic Pullman District (above), is a remnant of railroad-car maker George Pullman's "model town" in South Chicago. Its corner-stone is the Queen Anne-style Florence Hotel, built in 1881 and named for Pullman's favorite daughter. The nonprofit Historic Pullman Foundation operates the hotel—which is owned by the State of Illinois—as a museum and restaurant. The baron and his family used the Pullman Suite (right) when they visited from their Prairie Avenue home. OVERLEAF: Chicago sculptor Lorado Taft designed the Fountain of Time. It was dedi-cated in Hyde Park, near the University of Chicago, in 1922. The haunting statue's theme, suggested by a line from Austin Dob-son, reads: "Time goes, you say? Ah no, alas. Time stays. We go."

Stately Hyde Park
(above and right)
owes its splendor to
the founding of the
University of Chicago
in 1892 and the devel-
opment of the World's
Columbian Exposi-
tion nearby a year
later. The fair
included a Midway
Plaisance that formed
the southern edge of
the university's
original campus. The
University of Chicago
is arranged in Gothic
quadrangles in the
manner of British
residential colleges.
Hyde Park and
adjoining Kenwood
went through a period
of decline and deterio-
ration, and a massive
urban-renewal project
obliterated theaters,
music clubs, and
historic houses with
artists' garrets.
But quality buildings
replaced them,
and the ultimate
result was the neigh-
borhood's return
to grandeur.

I'M COMING FROM HOME AND I'M GOING TO THE UNIVERSITY. I COME FROM MODEST BEGINNINGS, FROM THE WORKING CLASS, AND WHERE I'M GOING I'M NOT SURE; I COULDN'T REALLY TELL YOU

FROM A CHURCH TO A CHURCH.

WE'VE BEEN HAVING A CONVERSATION ABOUT HOW TO INTERWEAVE THE STORIES OF GENESIS AND EVOLUTION.

I'VE COME FROM THE NORTH SIDE TO MEET A FRIEND WHOSE FAMILY I'VE KNOWN FOR TWENTY YEARS. HE'S A YOUNG MEXICAN IMMIGRANT. AFTER LUNCH, I WENT TO SEE THE SCHOOL WHERE HE GOES TO STUDY ENGLISH AND THEY HAVE PEOPLE FROM OVER THIRTY COUNTRIES THERE. I KNOW HIS FAMILY BECAUSE THEY ARE AZTEC SPEAKERS IN MEXICO. I MET THEM BECAUSE I'M STUDYING LINGUISTICS AND AZTEC LANGUAGE. YOUNG MAN DOESN'T KNOW THAT LANGUAGE. NEVER HAD ANY REASON TO USE IT. SO MAYBE HIS JOURNEY FROM THE NORTH TO THE SOUTH I'VE COVERED A LOT OF GROUND, THE NORTH TO THE SOUTH SIDE OF THE CONTINENT.

HOME, PROBABLY BE QUIET WITH MY WIFE AND KIDS.

I'M TRYING TO OPEN UP MY OWN BUSINESS.

FROM WORK AT THE MUSEUM. I'D SAY I WAS JUST ABOUT BLAND, I WOULD SAY. I HOPE IN MAYBE HALF A YEAR IT'LL BE SUPER WONDROUS. I'LL BE OUT OF THIS CITY THEN, OUT WEST, LITERALLY AWAY FROM ALL THIS FUNK.

HOME, AHH, PROBABLY TO WARMED OVER DINNER FROM TOMORROW.

WELL, RIGHT NOW OUR CHOIR IS GETTING READY TO DO SEVEN LAST WORDS, MUSICAL VERSION OF THE BIBLE AND WE'RE WORKING VERY HARD ON THIS.

THE SEVEN LAST WORDS WERE HIS LAST WORDS BEFORE HE DIED ON THE CROSS.

IT IS FINISHED.

WHERE AM I GOING?

I'M STILL TRYING TO FIND OUT.

IF THINGS ARE NOT GOING THE WAY YOU WANT, YOU HAVE TO MAKE IT BETTER OR JUST GO ON FROM THERE.

ALL THE
I FEEL BE
HERE, WA
AROUND
PARK IN
SPRING,
THE CHA
OF GOING
TO SCHOO
THIRTY Y
HAS CON
FOR ME T
IS MY CA

I HOPE TO BE GOING UP SOMEWHERE IN THE WORLD.

The mural contains the following partially visible text:

U GOING?

ARN MORE ABOUT
D HOPE TO GAIN
AND THAT'S
I CAN ASK

I GOING TO?
ONOMIST.
TING REAL SOON
ING TO GET OUT
E...LIVING
REAL WORLD,
IG AWAY FROM
CLOISTERED
RONMENT.
GOING TO MISS
THERE CHICAGO
NOT GOING TO MISS
WN HERE.

IS PART OF THIS
RESSING FEELING
VE TO WALK THIS ROUTE
RYDAY AND IT'S LIKE
JAIL CELL
D OF MENTALITY.

NOT THE MOST
PORTUNE TIME
DISCUSS WHERE I'M
ING SPIRITUALLY
EAN, I'M GIVING
MINAR ON GROWTH
EORY. I'M ON
OTHER PLANE
TOGETHER.

HOPE THE PROPOSED MURAL
NOT DEPRESSING LIKE IT IS NOW
THINK THIS INTEGRATION IDEA IN
HE MURAL ACROSS THE STREET IS
BIT HITTING PEOPLE OVER THE HEAD.

I'M A YOUNG PERSON
AND I'M JUST TRYING
TO STRUGGLE AND SURVIVE
IN THE WORLD AND
JUST LIVE THE
AMERICAN DREAM,
JUST THE STEP BY STEP
STRUGGLE OF GOING
FROM BEING SMALL
AND NOT HAVING
ANY SUCCESS TO SUCCESS.

I'M FROM THE ENGLEWOOD
DISTRICT. IT'S REALLY
HARD THERE. IT'S A LOT
OF PEOPLE OVER THERE
WHO DON'T TO SUCCEED
IN LIFE AND TO BE SOMETHING
IN LIFE. BUT IT'S A LOT OF OTHER
PEOPLE AROUND THEM WHO DON'T
WANT THAT MAKE IT HARDER FOR
THE GOOD PEOPLE TO BREAK
THROUGH THE CHAINS AND
DO SOMETHING WITH THEMSELVES.

I SEE A LOT OF RACISM AND STUFF
WHAT A LOT OF STUFF THAT HOLDS ME BACK
FOR THE COLOR I AM. WE ARE ALL
HUMAN BEINGS, SO IT SHOULDN'T
REALLY MATTER. BUT YOU CAN'T TELL
SOME OF THE PEOPLE THAT.

"Public art" turns up in surprising places, including an "El" station on East Fifty-sixth Street. On this rather existential mural (left), people of diverse backgrounds address the question "Where are you going?" with answers such as, "Home, probably to be quiet with my wife and kids," and "It's not the most opportune time to discuss where I'm going spiritually. I mean, I'm giving a seminar on growth therapy. I'm on a different plane altogether." ABOVE: On South Lake Park Avenue, the Chevrolet Building, which once housed an automobile dealership and was dramatically saved when most of the block was razed, includes beautiful terra-cotta details.

A gaggle of gargoyles adorns an entry gate to the University of Chicago (opposite), which sprawls across 184 acres of South Chicago. The university's medical, law, economics, and graduate schools are world-renowned. ABOVE: O'Gara and Wilson antiquarian booksellers in Hyde Park, near the University of Chicago, is known city-wide as a likely place to locate used and scarce scholarly books. OVERLEAF: The Museum of Science and Industry, the grande dame of Chicago's thirty-four museums, was built as the Palace of Fine Arts at the 1893 world expo. Its exhibits include a replica of a coal mine, a "whispering gallery," the Apollo 8 spacecraft, and the workings of a German submarine. Kids and adults alike gravitate to the Omnimax Theater, where movie scenes reach out and surround them, and to a pulsating, sixteen-foot model of the human heart.

Index

This neighborhood, about fifty blocks north of downtown, typifies the city's outer edge, just inside the suburbs. Many two- and three-bedroom brick homes, built in the 1940s and '50s, have been individualized with additions and prized plantings. Neighborhood kids are Chicago sports diehards in training, whose garb depends on the sport in season.